On Rock Bottom and Know Where to Turn

Allan Jones

Order this book online at www.trafford.com
or email orders@trafford.com

Most Trafford titles are also available at major online book retailers.

Printed in the United States of America.

ISBN: 978-1-4907-2870-4 (sc)
ISBN: 978-1-4907-2869-8 (hc)
ISBN: 978-1-4907-2871-1 (e)

Library of Congress Control Number: 2014903770

Trafford rev. 03/03/2014

 www.trafford.com

North America & international
toll-free: 1 888 232 4444 (USA & Canada)
fax: 812 355 4082

This is a book which is hard to write. The reason being it is a subject, that a lot of people have thought about and this topic is suicide.

During adolescence, I believe a large number of males and females, ponder the thought of what is the purpose of life. Why am I here? Is life worth living?

In young adulthood the same questions may arise. Sometimes there are different circumstances, negative circumstances such as the loss of love.

Even the word, "suicide" itself is void. It sends shockwaves through your mental and physical being. Has life dealt you a wrong hand of cards?

Would it be romantic to do it, meaning that you would be remembered as an icon, would that not be twisted thinking. To me it would be, the ultimate sin.

By no way should anyone take their life. I have to say this at the beginning of the book for the simple reason, please do not suicide, for what ever meaning or reason. It is not justifiable. Life as we know it has it's ups and downs. To take your life can be viewed as many things. Which are definitely not good. What is making me write this message, it is simple my older brother did it. Yes seven years of age difference.

As I keep on writing about it we will dig deeper and deeper into life and death. My mom and dad fell apart! My relatives fell apart! His female partners fell apart! I fell apart!

Sure you might think that his suffering was over but our suffering just began.

First off, you think, are the police right about this. Did he actually kill himself? Did he have enemies we did not know about? Did he get into to deep with the wrong people? The questions go on forever.

You analyze his life, in depth. You say to yourself I am going to look into this. We are going to find the answers. We are going to take this apart piece by piece.

You cry and cry and then get angry and cry some more.

We live in such a complex society the reason being, I believe, is do to the advent of medical advancements, technical advancements, such as computers, and multi tasking. Yes the pressure is on. You go to work, but first you have to get there and hope that there is no road rage. You say to your neighbour good morning and the next thing you know is that you are racing with him to get to work, a part of road rage.

I do not want to get off topic but society is moving much to fast. The wars that rage, the indifference that man holds against each other. We must take a snap shot of this, look at it carefully. Can we slow it all down. Put things in the right perspective. I believe that everyone has to take a deep breath and say calm is in order. Yes there are things that we just have to experience and continue to move forward irregardless of the stress and strain.

In my personal life I have experienced many traumas. But these traumas just made me stronger and to continue with the fast pace of life.

Yes my brothers name was Dennis. He was born January 25, 1952. Like I said before he was seven years older than myself. His story I hope will live well past my natural life. What makes a person take their own life? We can look at circumstances. We could look for reasons. We can look at his mental health, his physical health and his spiritual life.

I think that when a person is in such despair they get into despair. It is like they have tunnel vision. All they can see is a way out of life. I would also like to say I believe not all people that commit suicide are mentally ill. The reasons are vast why a person would take their own life.

Human beings are not perfect, we make mistakes. Let us go a little deeper with it. Dysfunctional families are abound. This is my personal opinion, but the family unit for some reason can become angry with each other, and because of unconditional love still stay together for the simple fact of forgiveness.

Suicide I think is a very personal choice. Deep in the loins of the person. The giving away of personal items. The final letter. With Dennis there were two letters. They were two renditions of songs. The first one was, "House Of The Rising Sun," by Eric Burdon and The Animals. The second one was, "If I Had Jessie's Girl," by Rick Springfield. This was discovered at the place of his residence. Also found was his family photo album. I sat there in this apartment with my mom and dad thumbing through the pages of that family photo album, thinking what a shame. My parents were at odds. It was a basement apartment. The landlord lived upstairs. The 12 gauge shotgun was taken by the police. Dennis had this maple wood chessboard that I kept. When I was back home again, I burnt my name on the back of it with a soldering iron. His electric guitar went to my younger brother. He did not have much in that apartment. I guess he hit rock bottom and no where to turn.

In this book I talk about the pain's of life and suicide. Why, because it hurts. The ones you leave behind cry out to the moon and the stars. Why did you do that? I loved you with all my heart and you tore it all apart. The shock, the tears, the anger.

Let me tell you about the anger. Dennis left behind two very young boys. These boys on hearing the news about their father hide under their beds, crying and trembling, with the question what did daddy do.

*Now to tell you a little about myself. Unfortunately at age 13 I was committed to a mental health facility. The reasons being, as the doctor said I had schizophrenia. Today I have to disagree with that diagnosis for the simple reason at 13 I had trouble sleeping and depression. How do I know that the answer is simple, at age twenty five I did develop schizophrenia, a full blown case of it. Hearing voices, no sleep, no appetite and no energy.

Then at 15 years of age I suffered another trauma. Yes I started working for this person, if you can call him that, and he raped me, then he tried to kill me by trying to run me over with his truck. I had to jump into the ditch to save myself.

Well back to the sanatorium for another six months. Also eight shock treatments to bring me back from my depression. Yes I still did not have schizophrenia. It seemed as though it was my fault, can you handle that.

The injustices in life are great. Here I am trying to make some money to go to high school, when this goof of an employer sodomizes me, tries to run me over with his truck and I end up in the san!

Any way Dennis and his friend Jerry, and my friend too, did not kill him but scared the living shit out of that thing that attacked me. Good!

Now back to Dennis, seeing since he is the main focus of the book. He was a blue baby when he was born, but he made it through it. When I came along he was seven years of age.

When I reached the age of 17 Dennis and I started to hang out together. He was 24 years of age. Had his second woman after his divorce to his first woman, which he had two sons with her.

Drinking booze, and smoking pot like it was going out of style. Now we were having a lot of fun, as long as he stayed away from hard liquor, which made him want to fight.

Myself I was a happy drunk, meaning I loved to party with out fighting.

For a few years we worked together at the same place. It was hard work but paid well. Friday nights would come and party time as well.

Yes Dennis and his second women where doing alright. She had a child from another marriage and that child grew up to be a doctor. Just goes to show that no one knows what the future has in store.

So here we are the Jone's brothers, high on life and going for it.

It takes me back when he and I built that second motorcycle. A 650 cc Triumph Bonneville. We had to tear down the whole bike. Sanded the frame, cleaned the chrome, put some new rubber on it. When Dennis kicked it over when we were done rebuilding it, the flames came out of the cross over pipes through the shortie mufflers. Yes our dad timed it right, because it sounded good and mean. The colour of it was candy apple blue.

Come on Dennis let us paint the town red. Let us pick up the boys and do some real partying. In this small town word gets around the Jones brothers are in town.

Once in a while I would have to hold Dennis down and cool him off, for he wanted to fight. We did not hurt each other to badly. You see now some of the reason's why he was drinking heavy. The loss of his first wife and their two boys worked on him yes a marriage that went bad.

His second marriage or common law woman lasted a few years. There again the fighting it did not bother me that much. As long as I could take him. Take him and pour him into his bed.

Now for another garage tale. Yes it was a Dodge Fury the 383 engine in it was shot. We changed it up to a 351 Ford Cleveland engine, yes strapped to a four speed Hurst Shifter and then 4:11 rear end gears. Needless to say it moved.

You see Dennis and I loved each other as brothers should. The pain he went through was large.

We moved around a bit because of the way jobs were. Down south up north what ever and where ever a person could make a buck.

Let us change gears now and go into the abyss that Dennis fell into. I remember going down south to visit him while he was with his second love. A week or so before I got there. He got thumped, busted nose, black eyes, broken jaw. I was with one of my down south buddies that I teamed up with before seeing Dennis. He was a mess. Mark and I looked at him and laughed. But it was not funny. So we sucked down a few browns and all three of us started laughing it up again. I mocked him with his wired up jaw as I mumbled as if my jaw was wired up too! I know we have native in us because Dennis and his drinking made him wild. This is not to take away from the native people. On one of our terrors I bumped into some guys that had some beer and

Dennis and I would trade them up for a bag of pot for some beers.

Oh no it went sour, they searched our truck for pot. We got pistol whipped, they ripped us off. I knew where they lived, the night was not over.

Went to where they lived and knocked on the door. We could hear laughing inside the house. One of them answered the door. I said to him hello we are here for our case of beer. They started to cry and we told them not to pistol whip any one anymore because it hurts. So we left and said just another night.

While I am on the topic of heavy duty. Dennis had words with me. We totaled the apartment. I ripped the natural gas heater off of the floor, pipes and all and through it at him! Well the place filled up with gas and I told Dennis not to turn any light switches on or off because the whole place would blow up!

So here comes the police and the fire department, we paid dearly for that night of drinking.

On a lighter note I have been clean and sober for over twenty years or more, and I thank God for that. You see it is very easy to find trouble even if you are not looking for it. And I stopped looking for it and it stopped looking for me!

Suicide is a dangerous act. What happens if it is uncompleted that is right, what happens if for instance that you try to swallow a gun, you put it into your mouth, you pull the trigger, blow off the side of your face but still live. Now you look disfigured for the rest of your life.

Now that every one stares at you because you are disfigured try living with that.

Did you take enough pills? Oh you did not and now you are blind. Trying to OD or overdose and that fails then what. Your intelligence is totally mixed-up. Then what? Of course you get the picture. The ones you leave behind are in constant pain and sorrow asking the question why.

With Dennis he lived while being transported to hospital via ambulance. That 12 gauge shotgun was his end. I will get into detail what he did as told to us by the police. This is by no means to glorify his death. First he used a fishing rod to activate the trigger. The shell or load in the shotgun was an SSG. The recoil of the shotgun broke his arm.

He blew away the right side of his heart and the left side of his right lung. That is enough for now about that. Oh just one more thing, he told the doctors at the hospital, just to let him die.

There are all kinds of ways to take your life but do not let me go over board with that. The people reading this book would have the understanding that enough is enough.

On rock bottom and know where to turn is the title of the book. I will try to give you insight into how to cope day by day with a mental illness.*

Suicidal ideations or in other words thoughts of self-harm or suicide are not permitted in this country or other countries.

My personal opinion of this is O.K., you are in crisis. You feel as though you are going to flip out. First step contact the people that are closest to you and you can trust them. If your family members cannot help you turn to people who can help. You see sometime care givers are your family and they can burn out.

For some people to ask for help is to be showing signs of weakness. My thought on that is forget about your pride and say please help me for I do not know what to do.

There once was this man who was an electrician. What happened was that he built a beautiful home. Well he insured it and then burnt it down to the ground to collect the insurance. Well the police charged him with arson. What did he do, he killed himself. I guess money was in that equation, but should it have been.

Like I said before money is just a monetary issue. I know we all need money to live that is a fact. Everyone that knew him knew he was a good person and he was. But this thing with money ruins a lot of people.

These are some examples of people in dire straits. As civilized people how do we approach people who are not themselves, due to illness, poverty, homelessness, love lost, addictions, all the human frailty that can be put on a person.

Now let me talk about the higher power, God, Jesus, the Holy Spirit. Yes we need someone or something to believe in.

I have made plenty of mistakes in my life, but to bad for me life goes on and it does. I will speak with empathy not with sympathy. What has my mental health issues done to me? It made me talk to other people with mental health issues. Dennis never had a diagnosis of a mental illness. How I loved my brother through the good and the bad. I have almost completely wasted my life crying about Dennis. But luckily I have my kid brother and kid sister.

I just wish my mental health was better. To change my medications. To change my life style, you have to try everything out, if something fails try something else.

We need certain things in life to survive, some are basic and some are complex. Let us deal with the complex issues. A relaxed state of mind and body. Thought processes that are changed from being negative into positive affirmations. With your internal self-talk, say things that are good about you!

Leave the past behind. Create a new life for yourself. If the people that say they are friends of yours well make sure that they are telling the truth.

So far in Canada we still have a health care system, but is it breaking down. Are mental health facilities being closed.

I try to be proactive with the mental health system as a whole. What is happening in this country, we are facing a lot of economic uncertainty. So is the rest of the world. Yes we should try to stay positive about it all, find our own peace, and just keep on going.

This book has to be written to lift up your spirit or spirits. I would like to tell you a joke, but I do not think that would do it. Right now it is hard to say it will be alright. This is me pondering that, not you. For you I hope that your life can change for the better.

I do not like the doctor's drugging little kids with prescription drugs like Ritalin when their brains are not fully developed. I am not a doctor, but do you need to be!

Is it true that sanatorium's may become thing's that are of the past? Putting people on the street because there are no more new monies that the federal, provincial, and municipal governments cannot afford. I hope that is not the truth, the reason being certain individuals need those services.

Man, my heart goes out to those that are homeless. I know because I came close to becoming one. What is it with people anyway they just walk on right by and ignore their fellow man.

I really believe that God created all of us as being equal. I guess when we get to meet Him we will surely know what the score is. Heaven or hell, here we go.

I could not believe it when I went on the web to the Wikipedia encyclopedia site and under the topic of suicide, they had a picture of the Golden Gate Bridge which has a telephone line straight to a suicide prevention hot line. So please do not jump off the bridge, thank you!

I must admit that I did try to commit but was unsuccessful. Thanking the Lord God that I did not. If you are thinking of it, suicide is not the answer.

Go out and trust someone and I mean now. When Dennis did it the Jones family found themselves in the eye of a hurricane, what a mess that was. Like I said before suicide is not the answer and it is not.

My dad blamed himself for it because he had bought Dennis the shot gun. Everyone one told him it was not his fault for buying that thing. I told him dad, Dennis would have found another way to check-out.

We have to count our blessings you see in undeveloped countries there is no mental health systems. The reasons being they cannot afford it. I have it on good authority, from my publishing consultant that their mental health system does not work well.

I am on page 37 of the rough draft. Think, think, think, is all I do. See this is the illness in me. The medications I take can possible cause this in me. This I do not know. But does anyone really know how the human brain fires.

I have permission from www.cchr.org; Citizens Commission on Human Rights International, which I am a member of. There has been a lot of misery and pain dealt out to people diagnosed with a mental health problem.

If you would go to; Citizens Commission on Human Rights International web site, it is up to you to decide for yourself what you think about their information. Personally I am not endorsing or condemning CCHR for I am pro-active when it comes to it. Yes I can say I sit on the fence looking at all things that concern the well being of everyone irregardless of being a patient or a mental health worker. Why, the answer is simple, we are all human beings.

This brings me to another story. She had just moved to town. She was a psychiatric nurse by profession. She started at the hospital. A couple of months went by. Yes she committed suicide. Do to the laws of the land. Meaning confidentiality none of the patients could say goodbye. Now do you understand what I am trying to say?

She was a person just like anyone else. I was told she had children, yes everyone cried in their own way. That is why I sit on the fence and look at the whole picture.

Now I am in such great pain. Both physically and mentally. The physical part of it has to be because or could be because the taking of prescription medications for so many years.

Mind wise I lack in all areas. You cannot be taking strong medications, without having side effects.

Now to go on to say about harm to ones self or harm to others. Look it, I would check out before hurting anyone, I do not want to sound contradictive, but if it came to the wire, I would have to commit. I do not want to be two-sided about this. I have talked to a lot of people about this and they themselves said the same thing. Talk about having your back against the wall. But come on if you are having extreme thoughts of suicide and or homicidal thoughts you had better phone the authorities and quick!

Now the question is are the medications causing these unwanted thoughts. Can anyone answer these pointed questions.

In my first book, "The Book Of Al" I told my life story. Now more people are telling their stories. How mental illness has pretty well mixed up their lives. I know first hand for the simple truth I suffer from the disease, "schizophrenia".

Just had the orkin mad in to check for bed bugs. Yes that is right, it is my living condition and it is better than being on the street. At lest their is no other vermin, not yet anyway. I do not complain because things could be worse. This can happen to any-one.

Time comes around when you are on the top of everything, then the next thing you know you are on rock bottom.

You have to ground your shelf, in reality. Take a good look around see what is right and what is wrong. Take the bad and change it for the good. The positive is there, you have to find it. Sometimes things will fall into place and you will feel good about yourself. Once this starts to happen, go with the flow. You are worthwhile, you are a good person.

When the bad thoughts come, look at them and disregard. Say to yourself this will pass and it will. Have faith in yourself for you are the one that can change things. Sure let me also say along the way you will meet other people that will help you, once you gain their trust.

Now, I have permission from Mary Ellen Copeland PhD. of the W.R.A.P. Program (Wellness Recovery Action Plan). I completed her program on July 10 2012.

It was offered by NISA (Northern Initiative for Social Action) it is an organization that I have belonged to for 14 years. Now back to the W.R.A.P. Program, I would recommend it to people that do not even have a mental health issue that is how strong I believe in Mary Ellen's program.

That is about all I can think of for now about Mary Ellen's beautiful program. The W.R.A.P. Program.

Now pain in and out. Sometimes I can hardly handle it. As you get older these health problems happen. On that brings me to another story. A neighbour of mine told me about the golden years. At that time I was young and spry. Now I am 55 years of age and saying the golden years are coming for me and they are.

The elderly also take their lives. Sad after a long life of struggle and strain and happiness and love. What can be done for them, besides praying and praying.

Do you believe in God, I do. When you have no one on this earth, God can be your best friend, please let Him be your best friend!

Dennis stopped by Christmas time all dressed up. Why was he all dressed up, was he trying to say good-bye. You look at all these things and ponder about it.

I try to be uplifting to the people that are reading this book. Trying to say never give up. Roll with the punches and get on with the show. Being busy is a good thing. It helps clear your mind of all the bad stuff!

If you have children comfort them. One of my problems with my girls was hoping they would not have my disease develop in them. But unfortunately my eldest did. You know what she is doing now? Her PhD in Psychology. My younger one has finished her 4 year Arts Program in the Arts, to become a teacher. Now is that not great, I think it is!

Winter time is rolling around the corner. Time to start going to out of the cold. Where they serve everyone like kings and queens. Your tables are served by waiters and waitresses. The food is good. The company is great. If you think I fell off a banana boat you are wrong. I thought in college. I am a qualified diesel mechanic. Once a married man for 25 years. The father of two girls. While I was young and single I was wild. There was nothing I would not do for a laugh! In the good sense of the word.

Now what are you going to do? You have a handicap. Everyone does. You see there was only one perfect one and we nailed Him onto a tree 2000 years ago. Yes that was Jesus Christ.

The first book I wrote took 3½ years to write. This was when I was living at a group home, run by CMHA (Canadian Mental Health Association). The total time I lived there was over six years. As my luck goes this group home was right beside the district jail. The jail was my home a couple of times due to drunk driving. This was many years ago, like I said I have not drank for over twenty years. My first impaired at age 19 was stupid because I was stupid. Simple as that.

My second impaired was after Dennis's death. Man I was crazy with anger. Like I am a mechanic, so guess what, yes that is right. I had one mean machine for a car.

I was told by John, Dennis's landlord upstairs that he would tell me what happened that night when Dennis died. I never made it down south. You guessed it the O.P.P. seen my massive burn out. The officer followed me and the hitch hicker I picked up for company. The lights came on and I stopped. The officer told the hitch hicker to find a new ride.

Come on Mr. Jone's time for your breathalyzer. I blew over 0.08. I never did make it there to talk with John about what happened that horrific night. I think it probably was not meant to be.

I would love to say growing up in this city of mine was good. At different times, times were good. At other times, times were bad. So as the story goes, if life has given you lemons, make lemon aid! I just thought I would add that one because it is the truth! Just like saying laughter is the best medicine, well it is.

O.K., time to get serious again. I have been jailed and I have been forceable confined to psychiatric hospitals, for a lot of my life. Jail because of the anger of drunk driving. The legal system did their job. Which was the right thing to do. If you break the law, expect to pay the price. If you have spent a lot of time in psychiatric hospitals do not think you have failed. It is just another feather in your hat. Take what you need, that helps you and leave the rest behind.

Did I become a goody two shoes. Yes I did. If I did not change my life style I would not be here, just that simple.

Let us suppose you are, for the first time in your life need help with your mind and thoughts, because after all this is the most important part of us. When it goes away, fear settles in, you think you are losing your mind. You are not. Our brains have pathways. Like I said before I am by no means a doctor.

Now you know you need help, so go for it. Through and through how serious is your thought process. Do you want to die? Who wants to die. No one really wants to die.

I have suicidal thoughts 80% of my waking day. That does not mean I will do it. Why. How would the people that love me feel? You got it. The way I felt when Dennis did it. It freaked me out so bad that I flipped out. But did not take my life. You should not take your life. I know it is hard. Life is hard even if you were born with a silver spoon in you mouth. Unfortunately it does not matter if you are rich or poor, tall or short, big or small. Get the picture, right on.

These pathways need to be reprogrammed. Sometimes medications help but sometimes they do not. If you can feel better with out medications than with. The more power to you. What ever does the trick. Search and search and search. Find the answers. Look into everything, I had too. Alternative medicines instead of toxic drugs which they are and I have been on them for years. I have to be because I am hooked to them.

I should practice what I preach and at times I do not, such as with exercise which should be done regularly. Reason I do have physical health problems so I do not exercise like I should.

Woke up this morning put on my photo album CD in the blu-ray DVD player. As the pictures change automatically. I just sit and stare at the photo's of the Jones family. Of course I see my dad and my mom. Dennis, Linda, Robert and myself, Allan.

Times have a way of changing. As we grow older our body and brain change. Once the body stops growing at about 21 years of age, or sooner. The human brain still is learning.

Now if the brain is changing itself what is stopping us from not switching our thought processes instead of being depressed to being happy.

I believe that with cognitive behavioral therapy we can change our negative thought pattern to a more positive one.

Now back to the photo album those pictures, upon looking at them brings warmth into my heart. Why, because I loved those people in the pictures and know them as my family, which they definitely are. Like the old saying goes, a picture tells a thousand words and they do!

Now back to Dennis. We were down south in the 4×4. Dennis was driving Wayne and I were passengers. Yes Dennis why don't we drive over the cliff with your 4×4 truck and kill us all.

When he started that devil may care attitude, and this was not the only time he played with danger, lives were at steak.

In my book, "The Book of Al." By Allan Jones. I tell about the time Dennis decided to lite a cigarette in the back of a truck, that had two 45 gallon drums, one of gasoline the other of diesel fuel. Well guess what, the truck blew up. How everyone made it out of there only God knows. Boy oh boy that brother of mine!

I will tell you how trauma affects a person's life. My example will be my grandmother (on my mom's side). In this story my grandmother is trying to get her mother's attention to tell her that their house was on fire. The very sad truth about this is that her brother was in the house. My grandmother never forgave herself because of that episode or whatever you would like to call that. I loved my grandmother with all my heart! She never forgave herself for that. The pain ran so deep inside of her. My poor grandmother, rest her soul.

Story time again. Dennis had his own rock and roll band when he was in grade 8. Amplifier, guitar and his vocals. They cranked out tunes like: Green Tambourine by the Lemon Pipers, Mr. Bojangles by

Nitty Gritty Dirt Band, and Wipe Out by the Surfaris.

They got together in our dad's garage and practiced day in and day out. While they played at school the principal came in to the gym and said it is to loud, the whole school can hear you. Everyone wanted their autograph.

We had a normal upbringing. My parents were very good people and hard working. Dennis also was a hard worker. He had to before he married at the young age of 17. He started with hard jobs, but then found some good work with a well known Canadian owned company. Unfortunately Dennis and a close friend of his got into trouble with the law and lost his job. This is when things went down hill for him. I believe he suffered from depression, but never seaked out help. We also have to consider the time frame.

Back in the late 60's and 70's the general population were not educated as they are today about mental health issues. I believe that there was one book that was written for the general public about self help. The book was called, "I'm OK You're OK" by Thomas A. Harris, M.D. Now we have a lot of books out there on mental health for self help. Hopefully my books will show insight into the abyss of mental illness. A first hand account of chronic schizophrenia which I suffer from.

Like I said in my teenage years I had depression and insomnia. I know this because now my mental health has deteriorated to such an extent as of hearing voices delusional thinking, fear of panic attacks and psychotic thinking.

I was told once that the human mind uses one tenth of it's potential. That makes me think can we harness that unused portion to better ourselves to have clearer thinking.

Back to Dennis with his sleep walking. They say not to wake up a sleep walker. Myself I have nightmares. They are vivid at times and then again they are not. At times we say that dreams are the soul of the mind. They reflect our inner being and I believe that.

With age comes wisdom and with wisdom comes hope and with hope comes life. That life is what you live. So live life to the fullest.

Now back to some more story telling. My brother Dennis and I were people not to be messed around with. We never took anyones life and that is a good thing.

The drinking was total foolishness, why we drank so much, was it do to the fact that both of us were self medicating. This does happen and maybe I do not have to tell you but alcohol is a depressant.

Any way back to some more story telling. Dennis was never charged with impaired driving. He did get charged with other offences like breaking windows and other small stuff. I thought that his drinking contributed to his acting out.

The last time I saw him alive he had black eyes. He was always invited in my home. He did not say how he got his black eyes, but I knew he was fighting again. We drank a little that night. In the morning he came into my bedroom and tapped me on the belly. I should have gotten up out of bed and said good-bye that morning for that is the last time I saw him alive.

The night before we drank a little, but not much! I clowned around with him about his black eyes and said, you look like a raccoon brother. We all laughed. If I would have known that was the last time I would see him, things would have been different or would they have.

Here we have it would, should and could. How it blew my mind and everyone else's mind. Dennis why did you do that.

Now I just sit in my apartment and think and think about that time over and over again. Now do you know why suicide is not the way to go. So I praise God each and everyday that I have.

We are living in desperate times. The year is 2013. I try my best to keep my hopes up. I believe we are living in the end times according to the Holy Bible. This is my opinion. I have read the King James Version of the bible four times and the New International Version once. To me a lot of the bible is graphic. The stories of people that do not follow God's word maybe forever dammed or will we all be saved by the blood of the Lord Jesus.

I have studied God's word most of my life and I believe it to be the truth. On rock bottom and know where to turn, turn to the Lord or your higher power or your spiritual being what ever helps you make it through the day.

Dealing with a mental illness is serious business and who ever has it should try everything possible to shake it. You know something it is the most important thing to do. What is life without having faith in yourself. Do you not remember in your youth that everything is possible. Have faith in yourself, I know it is hard but give yourself permission to take it easy. Yes give yourself a well deserved break.

There are people out there that are not mentally well and do not even know it. This is true. Maybe it is best that they do not know and everything happens for a reason.

As I look out side the first snow fall is coming down how the world looks so clean as every-thing is a new. If only all the days were a first snow fall.

Now back to reality, you will have to shovel the snow away. There may be government assistance programs you have over looked. Can you get back into education and up-grade your skills. Have you searched out voluntary or paid work. Also common sense and a sense of good humour go along way.

Myself I live on a fixed income and so may you. I know that is very hard at times to live on a strict budget, no kidding ah!

Organize you time and spend it well. If you have bad thoughts get busy doing something. The things that make you sad try looking at them in a different way. Turn it around.

Like I said I am 55 years of age, if you are a lot younger I have a story to tell you. At age 13, psychiatric hospital for six months. Then back on my feet for two years. At age 15 back to the hospital for another six months, not due to my fault. I suffered a trauma which I talked about in my first book.

I have to write these books for the simple reason my story has to be told. We can read all the books that professionals have written but have these professionals suffered from a mental illness. I would have to say a small number, maybe.

With me my mind has been completely bombarded with shock treatment or E.C.T. which is Electroconvulsive Therapy. Then by oral ingestion of psychiatric drugs to many to mention also by injection, of these same toxic drugs.

All the promotional advertisements we see for: antipsychotics, antidepressants and anti-anxiety medications are all seductive in nature.

I have mentioned before about www. cchr.org (Citizens Commission on Human Rights International). I believe them to be very proactive in the mental health field. Like I said, take it for what it is worth.

Now time for another story. I have not drank or smoked up for over 20 years. I will never touch the stuff. I do not believe that the booze or the pot has disabled me. Can you tell by the way I write that I am high functioning. Thank God for that.

I just had my first webinar, compliments of Trafford Publishing and the Author Learning Center. I find that my writing style is unique for the simple fact that I try to keep it simple and to the point.

Page after page I write free hand. The thinking of what to put down on paper is stashed deep in the crevices of my mind. My life story and the lives around me.

Out of the cold is on for tonight as we sit down for a free meal. The homeless in this town is large. What contributes to this I believe is the advent of complex technologies that are putting people out of work.

As the snow starts to fall winter is coming on. I am looking at all of these people from all ages. Babies, children, teenagers, young adults, adults, middle aged and senior citizen's, yes out of the cold is appreciated by all. Grace is said before the meal.

Back to some more story telling. Dennis and I were sleeping at our mom and dad's place, this was when both of us were brothers on the same side. We talked at length about life. The crosses that we carried. Dennis was of strong character and suffered some unbelievable traumas.

He got wiped-out with the Triumph Bonneville. While doing a wheelie, from where he worked, a car blew the stop sign and smashed right into him he lifted his leg in time and did not lose it. Then again he was going over a set of railway tracks and the throttle stuck wide open, he shut it down without incident. Then another time he is rushing home from work and the police had him on radar for speeding. Of course Dennis tried to outrun the officer but started to have mechanical problems. So Dennis pulled it over. The officer got out of his cruiser walked up to

Dennis and said, "What do you think you are doing." Dennis said, "The bike has a short in it." The officer said to Dennis, "I think you have a short in your head."

Dennis was not a bad person according to the trauma officer, down south, after his suicide. Really he was not that bad. Sometimes as people go the drinking and partying can get out of hand. Dennis did not take anyone's life but his own. As his brother I am here to tell you what hurt really is.

I tried to drink it away, smoke it up with pot. Relocated to a new place or ran away to try to leave my problems behind. None of that worked. What really will work is distraction, get your mind on to something else. Divert your attention to things that make you happy. Listen to music you like. Watch movies that are calming to you. Talk too close friends that have had similar experiences with life events. Talk to people that have had normal types of life experience, but they maybe far and few between for the simple fact that everyone has had negative life events because that is a part of life.

Yes bad ass Allan tried pretty well everything. Reason being I had to experiment with everything.

When at 13 years of age the system throws you into the mad house, it makes you think what the heck is going on here! I knew I could not sleep and I was down in the dumps. School became a chore it was not a fun thing that it should have been. I lost out of life back then. Let me tell you when they put you under the microscope and analyse you, you start to think when is this nightmare going to end. Back in 1971 the doctors were just scratching at the surface of mental illness. Not to mention the fact that they misdiagnosed me back then, with schizophrenia when all I had was depression and insomnia.

What a way to start your teenage years off. Then back to the hospital at 15 years of age because of someone else. Yes that is right, because of this goof that tried to run me over with his truck after assaulting me. I could have stabbed him with my knife or hit him with his own fire extinguisher that was in the cab of the truck. Not only did this animal hurt a child he took advantage of a mentally ill child. How do you like those apples. Yes depression and sleeplessness is a mental disorder.

Anyway let us go back to Dennis while we are drinking with the boy's. Yes some people can be peaceful drunks like me and some people like Dennis can be tyrants. Guns and alcohol do not mix well. Dennis sits with his back against the wall at the bar. We are told by other patrons that we cannot be there. Well the nerve of them telling the Jones brothers that we cannot drink there. So does a fight break out, sure it does. That was back in the day of the early 70's. Like I said before I have not drank for over 20 years. I had to stop reason being it was not going to bring Dennis back. I was crying in my beer. Messing up with the police and law and order. Never again would I drink and smoke up. This is a message about hope. This is a message about love. This is a message about courage. You see it takes more courage to be of sober mind than to be a drunken fool!

Did the drinking and drugging that Dennis was doing help him? The answer is definitely not.

My mother said to me, a number of years after Dennis's demise, that he was a coward that could not face up to the challenge's of life. Myself I loved him and so did my mom, but that was a strong statement to make. Definitely coming from a mother.

Now my dad on the other side of this mess was a loyal father. Dennis died in 1982. My father died in a car accident back in 1985, 3 years after Dennis's death. Could it have been that my dad was overstressed, had heart failure, went threw a red light and got T-boned. My father was never the same after Dennis's suicide. Blamed himself for buying that 12 gauge shotgun. Would dad still have beaten himself up if Dennis chose to play chicken with his car versus train and got killed in the process.

It is hard to know how my loving dad would have responded. That day, when mom phoned me about Dennis and what he had done all I could think about is going down south and bringing my parents with me to check it out.

To me the shock of it all blew my mind. I went on robotic mode separating mind from body and became a machine.

The first place we stopped was the cop shop. The trauma officer was very kind. We learnt that Dennis killed himself with the 12 gauge Ithaca pump shotgun. I do not know the reason why I go into depth about that fire arm. Could it be that that gun was used for his demise. Ithaca guns are top of the line in guns.

Let us just say for a moment a person takes their life. We ask the question, how did they do it. Is that like trying to put closure on the end of the person's life. Trying to grab some reason to it all.

I will tell you every thought you can think goes through you mind, when death comes calling.

Who is left behind, the family and friends. We can also state all the people that found out about his death, even

though they did not know him, their
minds focus on the event thinking
about their own place in life, should I
or shouldn't I if that person is unstable.
If he could do it I can do it. To do you
understand where I am coming from? It
sets up a poor example.

Yes page 91 of the manuscript. At times
I have to think about what comes next.
Will life get better for me here. I have
to concentrate on making it better for
myself.

Like I said I suffer from one of the most
dreaded mental illnesses, schizophrenia.
Yes it is the worst to have. Did Dennis
have it, no but I do believe he was
depressed.

You may have noticed that sometimes
I repeat the same event over but to look

at it from a different angle and also to get my point across.

Woke up again at 5:00 am. Put Netflix on to watch J. Edgar Hoover. Thinking and thinking again. It is November 25 2013. I have to get through another day. Will the hospital phone today for my pre-admission and admission to get my heart operated on. Pretty scary ah.

They will be cutting me from stem to stern or the long surgical way to get to that aorta and remove the bulge or as they say the aneurysm which has grown to 6 centimeters almost two and half inches.

Now even though I am suicidal I still do not want to die. This is what mental illnesses do to people. They think and think about death and dying. How can we change this. How can we change this thought process, that is the $65,000.00 dollar question.

Myself I try thought diversion. This is what you do. First off set the scene that you want to do. Take multiple things to occupy yourself. This will help take the voices away. If you are busy with distraction it will occupy your mind. Sounds like common sense well it is. I usually have a movie going. I am writing down thoughts. I am thinking about what I will be doing for the day. Some people keep daily journals. They keep writing and writing. Keep your hands busy. Build a plastic model. Draw some art. Do you get the drift.

You have to speak-up for yourself. If the medications are not working tell your doctor. Personally, at this time I would like to change psychiatrists but he will not allow me, this is not right. I have to look into this. But that is my problem, not yours.

You can not blame yourself for not feeling well, it is just one of those things. Look at the good things in your life. They are there, you just have to find them.

Now for paranoia. It can be devastating I know because I have it. The relentless feelings and thoughts of persecution, always having to use other people as sounding boards to check your sanity over and over again. Do not be ashamed if you can do this you are showing signs of reality. If you can not do this do not fear for the simple fact you are not ready yet or you would like to keep it to yourself, which also shows your intelligence. Oh yes you are!

For every one the mind plays tricks on us. Fascinating is it not. At times I have flash backs. The content of them are as follows they are negative in nature. Everything I did in my life was wrong. I made so many mistakes, were they all mistakes, no but the mind dwells on the negative. Like a computer that goes to default to keep operating even though the system stopped fully functioning. This is my best explanation that I could come up with.

Could not sleep anymore. At 4:00 A.M. I woke up again and started to write some more. Phoned the US of A warm line. Talked for a bit. Warm lines are a good thing. You are talking to a real person instead of a automated computer voice. Now that I say that, the crisis intervention program may become that automated system, hope not.

People need people, not machines talking to people. That computer is definitely heartless and could not care less about you.

I saw the depression in Dennis's eyes and took a picture of him. He was wearing his work clothes, you could tell not all was right with him. He was the strong and silent type. I wish he would have talked to someone, anyone.

The tears that we cried, oh Dennis I hope that the Lord above forgives you because I have. My craziness with him was kept to a medium. At the rate we were going with our drinking we were fortunate that no one ended up dead.

Now I am 55 years of age and I have learned a lot. Life is precious and should not be taken lightly. Here we are walking down the street avoiding the man or woman in the street as they ask for help. In the 70's it was rare to see this type of street person. Now the homeless people are all over the place. How do we fix this? There has to be an answer. The people in the street have mental and physical problems or maybe not because they have fallen between the cracks of the system.

Day in and day out I count my blessings, and thus far my prayers have been answered. The thought of being saved is great. To believe that Jesus died for our sins, paying the ultimate price, his life. I know at times that all people, even Christians fall from grace, believing or doubting the significance of the Lord Jesus Christ.

Dennis must have been at such a crossroad in his life that the only way out was to take his own life.

Now at this point in the book, how much more can I write about people that take their own life? Now to reread the book again and again. To try to give more insight into the act of suicide. What should be said about it.

Now for our emotions. Do we have to remain emotionless around people we do not know? Like putting on a false face in public. I have to at times, I wish I did not have to, but I do, we all do.

My mother said it like it is or was. She did not hold back when it came around to it. I guess being a French Canadian like she was, made her tough as could be.

My dear dad on the other hand was quiet and smart. He was a hard working man, that loved his family. A miner, a fire fighter and a veteran of the second world war.

Now to interrupt for I have something to write about that is important. The death of my workers' father. Yes on this day I went and got a sympathy card for my workers' family, because I know them.

Yes my worker is a registered nurse or R.N. He is very good at what he does for the simple fact I have had a lot of R.N.'s. And he stands out as one of the best.

Now back to work on the book. The books that I am writing are important to anyone involved in the mental health system, whether a consumer or a worker. Man I have had my share of it. Also knowing what I am talking about. For heaven's sake listen to me and what I write.

As I watch my flat screen a movie about Jesus himself which brings me joy knowing I am saved. Even for those God gave you free will to believe in him or not.

As I am getting older I find I know more and more about everything, as most people do and we learn from our mistakes which I have many.

Starting out this morning with some rock and roll music. I love listening to all types of music. Variety is the spice of life.

A little bit of this a little bit of that. I think back when I studied the bible, (The best selling book in the world) which I read five times, which really does not go with rock and roll music, but what ever turns you on.

Experiment with your life. Choose things that make you feel good. If it makes you feel bad, try it one more time to make sure it does not work. Then move on to something else.

You have to push your envelopes. I know it sounds hard, well it is, but do not give up. It is day in and day out.

I study everything and why not. If you are on disability it is a good way to keep busy. If you work the more power to you. Work is good for the self esteem. Studying is good for the self esteem.

You are a person and like most people you are good at somethings and not so good at others. Well join the rest of the world. The things you do that help you, keep on doing them. Common sense does go a long way.

I believe that the strengths you have should be built on, to further you on the road of life.

Printed in the USA
CPSIA information can be obtained
at www.ICGtesting.com
LVHW091235101123
763572LV00001B/49